Marion Bridge

Marion Bridge

Daniel MacIvor

[handwritten inscription:]
Dear Jane,
One show to
late — but
there's always
next time.
with great respect
David MacIvor

Talonbooks
1999

Talonbooks
#104—3100 Production Way
Burnaby, British Columbia, Canada V5A 4R4

Typeset in New Baskerville and printed and bound in Canada by Hignell Printing Ltd.

First Printing: May 1999

Talonbooks are distributed in Canada by General Distribution Services, 325 Humber College Blvd., Toronto, Ontario, Canada M9W 7C3; Tel.:(416)213-1919; Fax:(416)213-1917.
Talonbooks are distributed in the U.S.A. by General Distribution Services Inc., 85 Rock River Drive, Suite 202, Buffalo, New York, U.S.A. 14207-2170; Tel.:1-800-805-1083; Fax:1-800-481-6207.

The publisher gratefully acknowledges the financial support of the Canada Council for the Arts; the Government of Canada through the Book Publishing Industry Development Program; and the Province of British Columbia through the British Columbia Arts Council for our publishing activities.

Canadian Cataloguing in Publication Data
MacIvor, Daniel, 1962-
 Marion Bridge

 A play.
 ISBN 0-88922-407-2

 I. Title.
PS8575.I86M37 1999   C812'.54   C99-910223-0
PR9199.3.M3225M37 1999

for my sisters
Donalda, Ann, Valerie and Anna

Marion Bridge was first produced in September 1998 by Mulgrave Road Theatre, in association with da da kamera, in Guysborough, Nova Scotia with the following cast:

AGNES . . . . Jenny Munday
THERESA . . . . Mary Ellen MacLean
LOUISE. . . . . Emmy Alcorn
Voice of JUSTIN. . . . . John Dartt
Voice of KARA . . . . Janet MacLellan

Directed by Josephine Le Grice
Lighting by Leigh Ann Vardy
Set and Costumes by Janet MacLellan
Stage Manager: Judy Joe

The Setting

All of the action (with the exception of the last scene) takes place in a space that represents the kitchen of the family home. In the original production the kitchen was indicated by a table and three chairs on an empty stage and the only props used were those indicated in the script. This minimalist treatment proved to be very effective. There are four exits which indicate four separate off stage areas: (1) the living room and pantry; (2) the sisters' bedrooms; (3) the exterior of the house; and (4) the mother's room.

The Sound

It is essential that the television sound come from a speaker placed in the offstage area where the television is indicated. It would be unfortunate to have the television sound coming through the main theatre speakers.

The Characters

AGNES MacKEIGAN	the eldest sister, living in Toronto, actress/waitress
THERESA MacKEIGAN	the middle sister, a Nun living in a farming order in New Brunswick
LOUISE MacKEIGAN	the youngest sister, lives at home

ACT ONE

Scene One

*AGNES sits alone on stage drinking. A flask in her
bag; a suitcase beside her. She addresses the audience.*

AGNES:

In the dream I'm drowning. But I don't know it at
first. At first I hear water and I imagine it's going to
be a lovely dream. Even though every time I dream
the dream I'm drowning each and every time I
dream the dream I forget. Fooled by the sound of
water I guess and I imagine it's a dream of a
wonderful night on the beach, or a cruise in the
moonlight, or an August afternoon in a secret
cove—but a moment after having been fooled into
expecting bonfires or handsome captains or
treasures in the weedy shore it becomes very clear
that the water I'm hearing is the water that's rushing around my ears and fighting its way into my
mouth and pulling me down into its dark, soggy
oblivion. No captains, no treasures, no bonfires for
me, no in my dream I'm drowning. And then, just
when it seems it's over—that I drown and that's the
dream—in the distance, on the beach, I see a child.
A tall thin child, maybe nine or ten. And his sister,

younger, five. Then behind them comes their mother spreading out a blanket on the sand. It's a picnic. And beside the mother is the man. Tall. Strong. And broad shoulders, good for sitting on if you're five, or even ten. Good for leaning on if you're tired, good for crying on if you're sad. And he's got his hands on his hips and he's looking out at the water, and he sees something. Me. And he reaches out and touches his wife's elbow who at that very moment sees something too and then the children, as if they're still connected to their mother's eyes, think they might see the same thing. And with all my strength—if you can call strength that strange, desperate, exhausted panic—I wave. My right arm. High. So they'll be sure to see. And they do. They see me. And then all of them, standing in a perfect line, they all wave back. The little girl, her brother, their mother and the man. They smile and wave. Then the mother returns to her blanket and the basket of food she has there, the man sits, stretching out his legs, propping himself up on one arm, the little boy runs off in search of starfish or crab shells and the little girl smiles and waves, smiles and waves and smiles and waves. And then I drown. And that's so disturbing, because you know what they say when you die in your dream. Strange. But stranger I guess is that I'm still here.

THERESA enters.

THERESA:
Why are you sitting in the dark?

AGNES:
I like the dark, it's good for my complexion.

THERESA:
I thought you were going to have a nap.

AGNES:
Whatever.

THERESA exits briefly to turn on some lights.

THERESA:
"Whatever." Don't give me any of your Toronto talk.

AGNES:
Toronto talk? "Whatever" is not Toronto talk. It's a word. It's in the dictionary. Look it up.

"//" before the following lines indicates overlapping

THERESA:
//"Whatever." "Whatever."

AGNES:
//If there even is a dictionary here.

THERESA:
//What's "whatever" supposed to mean?

AGNES:
//The only book I ever remember seeing around here is the Bible.

THERESA:
//That's all you hear from the kids—"whatever"— and all that means is "who cares" or "I don't care." What kind of world is that?

AGNES:
//There's probably no dictionary here because I bet the Bible doesn't allow good Christians to have dictionaries. Too much information.

THERESA:
Nobody cares, that's why the world is in the mess it is. The whole world's gone "whatever."

AGNES:
Whatever.

THERESA:
How's everything here?

AGNES:
Fine. Where did you rush off to?

THERESA:
I told you. Mass.

AGNES:
Oh yes Mass. Sister Theresa, holier than Swiss cheese.

THERESA:
(*noticing the suitcase*) Have you not been upstairs?

AGNES:
I'm steeling myself for the journey.

THERESA picks up the suitcase and moves to exit.

THERESA:
I'm going to put you in Louise's room and she and I will take the little room next to Mother's.

AGNES:
It's got wheels.

THERESA:
What?

AGNES:
The suitcase has wheels.

THERESA:
Oh I'm fine.

AGNES:

It's got wheels.

THERESA:

I don't mind carrying it.

AGNES:

Use the bloody wheels! It's not a sin you know. You don't have to make every goddamn thing you do the way of the cross.

THERESA:

Are you drunk?

AGNES:

Drunk? What exactly is drunk?

THERESA exits.

AGNES:

Do you mean having had a drink? Or two? Or three? Is drunk measured by amount drunk or by the effects of the drinking? And anyway a lady never gets drunk a lady just ... relaxes. Loose women get drunk. And God knows I'm not a loose woman. Not that I haven't tried. But of course if I were drunk than how could I possibly answer you? I'd be too drunk to know if I were drunk wouldn't I? So I can't really answer that question: "Are you drunk?" But I could tell you how I feel; if I felt anything I mean. I don't think I've felt anything in some time, and I certainly don't think I'm feeling anything now. I don't think that's 'drunk' is it? I think 'drunk' is supposed to be a lot more fun than this isn't it? But then again why am I asking you? You've never been drunk have you? You've never been anything have you Saint Theresa?

THERESA returns.

13

THERESA:
    Mother's up.

AGNES:
    Mmmm.

THERESA:
    If you want to see her.

AGNES:
    I saw her.

THERESA:
    Oh.

AGNES:
    She was asleep.

THERESA:
    The pills put her right out.

AGNES:
    Mmmm.

THERESA:
    But she's up now. If you want to see her.

AGNES:
    Stop with the "If you want to see her"—of course I want to see her. What do you think I came here for? Not a bloody holiday that's for sure.

THERESA:
    Well I just—

AGNES:
    Don't pull any of your passive-aggressive bullshit on me, Saint Theresa.

THERESA:
    Pardon me?

AGNES:

(*mocking her*) "Mother's up if you want to see her." A slight emotional tremor in the voice—eyes slightly averted—fingers nervously picking at her skirt. I'll see her when I'm bloody ready. Christ.

THERESA:

As you wish.

AGNES:

First of all there's no one to meet me, then I've got to take the bus in from the airport—which alone and with luggage is a serious exercise in humility—then I'm not home fifteen minutes and you're rushing off to Mass and leave me alone here with Mother on her death bed. Welcome to Sydney.

THERESA:

Oh stop it.

AGNES:

Why do I let you do this to me?

THERESA:

Whatever's being done to you you're doing it to yourself.

AGNES:

There she bloody goes again.

THERESA:

Louise is home.

AGNES:

What?

THERESA:

She just pulled in.

AGNES:

Oh fantastic, now that you've got me in a state.

15

AGNES exits.

AGNES:
Christ bloody hell. Christly goddamn bloody hell.

THERESA:
Just calm down.

> *LOUISE enters. She holds a can of pop throughout the scene.*

LOUISE:
How's Mother?

THERESA:
A little restless.

LOUISE:
Agnes get in alright?

THERESA:
Yes fine.

LOUISE:
Where is she?

THERESA:
In the bathroom. So you got the car all taken care of?

LOUISE:
Oh yeah, it was just some buildup in the fuel line.

> *Pause.*

LOUISE:
She drunk?

THERESA:
Well she hates to fly.

LOUISE:
Mmmm.

THERESA:
    She's a little upset.

LOUISE:
    'Cause of Mother?

THERESA:
    I don't think Agnes thought she'd be quite so bad.

LOUISE:
    She went in?

THERESA:
    Well, not while I was here.

LOUISE:
    Did Mother get her pills?

THERESA:
    Yes.

AGNES:
    (*calling from off*) Who's that I hear?

    AGNES enters.

LOUISE:
    Hi.

AGNES:
    Oh God! Look at you! You put on some weight.
    That's good, your frame looks good with a little
    weight on it.

LOUISE:
    I'm just the same as always.

AGNES:
    It really suits you.

LOUISE:
    Sorry I didn't pick you up but the car's been giving
    me some trouble.

AGNES:

Oh that's alright, I love a nice bus ride.

LOUISE:

How you doing Agnes?

AGNES:

Wonderful. Just wonderful. I got involved with a little repertory company this winter who does these challenging little adaptations of Ibsen and Chekhov and Strindberg and so on—really interesting stuff— tart them up a bit, you know, the girls in black vinyl boots and big hair styles and the boys in little Speedo bathing suits, that sort of thing. Audiences just eat it up. And a really interesting take on the plays too, not just all flash and so on, a brilliant, brilliant director working with the company, really challenging man, really sharp mind. And a lot of film work, little things, good parts, nothing too gaudy—the problem with leads is that the supporting parts are so much better. Last week my agent offered me something, a second lead in an American movie of the week and honestly! I just said absolutely not, you couldn't pay me—couldn't pay me enough to do this. But me me me enough about me, how are you honey. Tell me everything. What's going on with you? How are you?

LOUISE:

Good.

Pause.

LOUISE:

Anyway I'm going to go have a minute with Mother.

AGNES:

Yes and then we'll sit down and have a nice long chat.

LOUISE exits.

AGNES:
My God what happened to her? Did she get a shock or something?

THERESA:
What do you mean?

AGNES:
She looks terrible, all puffy and strange.

THERESA:
She's fine, she's just herself. She's worried about Mother.

AGNES:
So you admit she seems strange.

THERESA:
Agnes, she is strange. She's always been strange. I don't know what you expect—you come home for the first time in how long? Years. And you expect everything to have turned into a movie or something. Everything's just the same as ever: Louise is strange, I'm a running the show and you're drunk. Same as it ever was except Mother's dying. Alright?

AGNES:
Alright.

Silence.

THERESA:
I've been here a week, it feels like a month.

AGNES:
Will you have a drink with me?

THERESA:

You're not serious.

AGNES:

There's always Mother.

THERESA:

Don't! Don't you dare. And she'll ask too. She wouldn't ask me but she'd ask you. But don't. It's very dangerous with the medication she's on.

AGNES:

I thought she couldn't talk.

THERESA:

She can't. Once it got into her thingy ... her larynx or whatsit she could only make these little squeaks but now there's no sound at all. That's why there's these.

THERESA removes a bunch of yellow post-it notes from her pocket. She shows them one by one to AGNES.

THERESA:

She's got all these various things she writes down. For 'yes' she writes a circle and for 'no' it's just a slash like this. If she wants a cup of tea she makes a 't.' A big 'H' means she's hungry and if she writes a little 'h' that's for Sandy.

AGNES:

Sandy?

THERESA:

It looks like a little 'h' but really it's a chair, because Sandy sits in the little chair when he comes over to read to her.

AGNES:

Sandy comes over?

20

THERESA:

He reads to her.

AGNES:

How is he?

THERESA:

I haven't seen him myself, this is all from Louise I'm
getting this. And don't throw the notes out. Louise
likes to save them.

AGNES:

I bet he's fat now.

THERESA:

Sandy? No!

AGNES:

I thought you didn't see him.

THERESA:

I didn't but Sandy was always taking such care of
himself. With his hair and his clothes just so and all
that.

AGNES:

Fat and bald.

THERESA:

That sounds less like a prediction and more like a
wish.

AGNES:

I've got no feelings for Sandy Deveau.

THERESA:

A squiggle like this means she has a headache—
don't ask me why but evidently that's the story. Just
give her a Tylenol—along with the regular
morphine. And a squiggle like this just rip up the

paper. I got this one a couple of times. It means she wants a cigarette.

AGNES:

She's not smoking?

THERESA:

She's only got half a lung.

AGNES:

Even less reason for her to quit.

THERESA:

No.

AGNES:

Oh come on let her have a cigarette.

THERESA:

Not. It's a sin. No, it's a crime. And if sin doesn't mean anything anymore well crime still does. Period. Alright. If she makes a dot, just a dot like that, that means she's got an itch. And sometimes ... I don't have one here, but sometimes if she's feeling all soft and lovey she'll make a little heart. She hasn't been doing too many of those. And 'P' is for pee.

AGNES:

For what?

THERESA:

Pee.

AGNES:

'P' for what?

THERESA:

For pee.

AGNES:

'P' what?

THERESA:

Pee, pee just pee.

AGNES:

Just 'P'?

THERESA:

Go PEE!

AGNES:

Oh.

THERESA:

And if she gives you a 'P' … well we'll get into that later.

AGNES:

She's not going to be giving me any 'P.'

THERESA:

Oh yes she will.

AGNES:

No, I'm telling you she won't be because I'm not doing that. I'm not a nurse.

THERESA:

Well neither am I, neither's Louise, but we still have to do it.

AGNES:

We'll get a real nurse.

THERESA:

She doesn't want a nurse.

AGNES:

Don't be ridiculous.

THERESA:
We'll talk about this in the morning.

AGNES:
Talk all you want.

LOUISE enters.

LOUISE:
Mother says you haven't been in to see her.

AGNES:
I was in.

LOUISE:
She says you weren't.

AGNES:
I'll spend the day with her tomorrow.

LOUISE hands a note to THERESA.

LOUISE:
Here.

THERESA looks at the note. She places it in her pocket.

THERESA:
Um hm.

LOUISE moves to exit.

AGNES:
Now where are you going? You sit down here with me.

LOUISE:
After. My show's on.

AGNES:
Forget your stupid old show! Sit down!

LOUISE:
For a minute.

AGNES:
So, now talk to me.

Pause.

AGNES:
Will you have a drink?

LOUISE:
I got a pop.

Pause.

AGNES:
So. Are you working?

LOUISE:
I got a job at the Red Rooster.

AGNES:
Right right, that restaurant.

LOUISE:
Pub.

AGNES:
Pub. How's that going?

LOUISE:
I got laid off in January.

THERESA:
I didn't like that place anyway.

LOUISE:
How come?

THERESA:
It was so loud.

LOUISE:
You were only there once.

THERESA:
 And what a night that was.

LOUISE:
 The Christmas party.

THERESA:
 Mother and I down in that … what was it a cellar or something. Dark! And loud! A fellow in a Santa suit with an accordion this far from my ear. Of course Mother was in her glory.

LOUISE:
 She did an excellent karaoke.

THERESA:
 My dear heavens. And the way she was carrying on with Santa Claus.

LOUISE:
 He started it.

THERESA:
 Well she's the one who got up on the table.

AGNES:
 Sounds charming. I'm so sorry I missed it. So Sandy's been by.

LOUISE:
 Now and then.

AGNES:
 How is he?

LOUISE:
 Just the same.

THERESA:
 She wants to know what he looks like.

LOUISE:
Just the same.

AGNES:
(*to THERESA*) I don't. (*to LOUISE*) How's his friend?

LOUISE:
Who?

AGNES:
Charles or whatever.

LOUISE:
Oh Charlie. Oh Charlie's, you know, just the same.

AGNES:
Do they still have the restaurant?

LOUISE:
Naw, closed that down. They opened up a gas station.

AGNES:
A gas station?!

LOUISE:
Sandy said people don't go out to restaurants anymore because they eat home.

THERESA:
Tell her the end of it.

LOUISE:
The end of it?

THERESA
The end of it. That Sandy said.

LOUISE:
Oh yeah, he goes: people don't go out to restaurants anymore because they eat home but you

can't get gas home—and then he goes: unless your mother's cooking.

THERESA and LOUISE laugh.

LOUISE:
But that was Charlie said that not Sandy.

THERESA:
Was it Charlie, oh of course I guess it would be, that Charlie's so bad.

LOUISE:
And you know what else!

THERESA:
What?

LOUISE:
He's over here, Sandy is, the other week and he's after me to join this bowling team they've got going.

AGNES:
Bowling?

LOUISE:
Imagine me bowling. That would be a laugh, me bowling.

AGNES:
Sandy bowling. That figures. Pinhead.

THERESA:
It would be good for you to get out a bit more.

LOUISE:
I'm not joining any bowling team. Especially because they play on Wednesdays and my show's on Wednesdays.

THERESA:
I thought your show was on tonight.

LOUISE:
I have several shows.

AGNES:
Louise!

LOUISE:
What?

AGNES:
Look at yourself.

LOUISE:
What?

AGNES:
What are you doing with yourself?

LOUISE:
Nothing.

AGNES:
Tell me something, tell me something new. What's happening? What's going on?

LOUISE:
With who?

AGNES:
With you.

LOUISE:
I don't know.

AGNES:
Well ... what are you thinking about these days? You must be thinking about something.

Pause.

LOUISE:
Um.

AGNES:
What are you thinking about?

THERESA:
Agnes ...

AGNES:
Louise? What are you thinking about?

Pause.

LOUISE:
Ryan's Cove.

AGNES:
Where's that?

LOUISE:
On TV. It started five minutes ago, that's why I'm thinking about it. It's going to be good too. 'Cause last week Mrs Ryan found out she had oil on this land she got left by this young guy Jake she was married to for a couple of weeks who she really truly loved but who died, and she doesn't want her daughter Kara to know that there's oil on the land 'cause she'd just sell it for the money, but Mrs Ryan doesn't want to sell it 'cause it's her only memory of Jake. See, Kara's really evil, right. Her boyfriend is Justin and he's really good, but Kara's just plain evil, but you're supposed to feel sorry for her because she's confused and has trouble with men. I don't feel sorry for her though. And now Kara knows that Justin has a gun, but he doesn't know he has a gun because he got it when he robbed the bank after he got hypnotized by Earl's cousin. Earl's cousin's not on the show anymore. They made him mean, and then they made him nice, and then they killed him in a car crash. Earl's cousin was really Earl, they had the same guy as both of them because they were

supposed to be identical cousins—which I never heard of. Did you ever hear of that, identical cousins?

THERESA:
Not really, no.

LOUISE:
Ah, they make half that stuff up I think.

Pause.

LOUISE:
Is our talk done?

AGNES:
Sure.

LOUISE moves to exit.

LOUISE:
It's going to be good, you want to watch it?

AGNES:
Maybe later.

LOUISE exits.

Pause.

THERESA:
Come on in and spend a little time with Mother.

AGNES:
No. Not tonight.

THERESA:
When then?

AGNES:
Not tonight.

THERESA:
As you wish.

THERESA exits. We hear a television program switch on in the next room.

JUSTIN: "Good lord Kara where did you get that gun?"

KARA: "It's not my gun Justin. It's yours."

JUSTIN: "That's impossible."

KARA: "See. Look. The registration is in your name."

JUSTIN: "My God Kara we've got to get rid of it."

KARA: "No! I have plans for this."

JUSTIN: "Kara what are you thinking? Are you insane?!"

KARA: "No Justin I'm not insane. I'm just bad. Born bad. Bad to the bone."

Alone on stage AGNES lifts her right arm high and waves. The light fades.

Scene Two

The next day. THERESA crosses the stage carrying clean sheets. LOUISE is in the living room watching a daytime talk show which we can hear. AGNES enters with shopping bags and a bouquet of flowers.

AGNES:
I give up! I honestly give up! I surrender to this town, I surrender, I give up! Look at these.

She heads toward the living room.

AGNES:

> Look at these.

> *She exits into the living room.*

AGNES:

> *(off)* Look at these!

LOUISE:

> *(off)* What?

AGNES:

> *(off)* Aren't they sad!

LOUISE:

> *(off)* They're okay.

> *AGNES re-enters.*

AGNES:

> I should say not! I marched all over town—and you
> wouldn't believe what they try to pass off as flower
> shops! Two stores didn't have a live flower in the
> place, just some god-awful arrangements of fake silk
> and feathers. And finally I find a place that has live
> flowers and this is what they give me! Have you ever
> seen such a sad affair! At home there are flower
> shops on every block, and tulips with heads as big as
> your fist. And this? This is two bouquets—I had her
> put two together to make this scrawny little thing—
> imagine trying to pass off a bit of hay and some wild
> flowers from the ditch as a bouquet. What I was
> really looking for was something special, something
> exotic. They don't get much more exotic here than
> those boring old African Violets—I asked the girl
> about Birds of Paradise and she recommended the
> pet store! Poor stunned little thing—ah well it's not
> her fault she hasn't been out of this crusty place all
> her life.

THERESA enters.

AGNES:

And wait 'til you hear about my adventures trying to find twelve grain bread.

THERESA:

What are those for?

AGNES:

For Mother's room. Do you want to bring them in?

THERESA:

Oh Mother doesn't like cut flowers.

AGNES:

What?

THERESA:

Oh yes, every time I ever tried to bring her flowers she'd get all sad because she didn't like to see them cut—she thought they should be left to grow.

AGNES:

I've brought her flowers before.

THERESA:

They'll just upset her. I know what—I know a place you can get gorgeous little pots of African Violets. She'd love that .

AGNES:

Christ.

THERESA:

And while we're on harping at you—because I know that's what you're going to think this is—

AGNES:

Oh I can't wait!

THERESA:

—And I know you don't like to be told what to do—

AGNES:

What?

THERESA:

Well ...

AGNES:

I should watch my language?

THERESA:

Actually, yes.

AGNES:

You're kidding? What did I say?

THERESA:

You don't know?

AGNES:

No, what?

THERESA:

The 'c' word.

AGNES:

The 'c' word? No I certainly have not used the 'c' word here!

THERESA:

Yes you ... Oh! No, not that 'c' word. Good heavens.

AGNES:

Well which 'c' word, there's only one 'c' word ... Oh well I guess that's a 'c' word too but I don't think I've had any cause to say that here either.

THERESA:

The Lord's name.

AGNES:

Oh—Right. I see. It's like that is it Sister?

THERESA:

It's not me—it's Louise. It bothers her.

AGNES:

Louise?

THERESA:

She started going to a prayer group. She takes it very seriously.

AGNES:

Louise?

THERESA:

She likes the people—and it's good she gets out. And I don't care what you believe or don't believe but prayer never hurt anyone.

AGNES:

So you've got poor Louise in the pack now.

THERESA:

It had nothing to do with me. It was her decision.

AGNES:

Next thing you know she'll be joining up with the Sister's of Saint E-I-E-I-O or whatever it is.

THERESA:

It's a little early for this isn't it? Or are you just getting going?

AGNES:

It's easy to hide away—what's hard is living a real life.

THERESA:

Look, just have another drink and calm down.

AGNES:

I'd a glass and a half of wine with lunch and that's—
What the hell am I explaining myself to you for?
Christ!

Silence.

THERESA:

Are you going to bring those flowers in to Mother?

AGNES:

I thought they'd just upset her.

THERESA:

They're very nice.

AGNES:

They're not very nice. I'll leave them here.

THERESA:

You've got to go in sometime.

AGNES:

God that television! (*yelling off*) Louise would you
turn that off!

LOUISE:

(*off*) I'm watching it.

AGNES:

(*yelling off*) Well mute it or something.

LOUISE:

(*off*) What?

THERESA:

Leave her be.

AGNES:

(*yelling off*) Mute it!

LOUISE:

(*off*) Mute it? It's a talk show! You can't mute a talk show!

AGNES:

(*yelling off*) Listen to some music or something!

LOUISE:

(*off*) It's my show!

AGNES exits to LOUISE.

THERESA:

Here we go.

AGNES:

(*off*) We just need a bit of a break alright.

The television is shut off.

LOUISE:

(*off*) Hey!

AGNES enters with the remote control. LOUISE follows close behind, she carries a can of pop.

AGNES:

I'm calling a time-out on the TV.

LOUISE:

Give me that back. It's my TV.

AGNES:

And it's my headache.

LOUISE:

Maybe you wouldn't have a headache if you weren't up all night drinking.

AGNES:

I was up all night because I couldn't sleep!

LOUISE:
You were up all night because it took you that long
to drink all Mother's arthritis brandy.

AGNES:
Get off my back.

LOUISE:
You drink so much it makes you stupid—and if
you're not drinking it makes you sick—and if you're
not sick or stupid, you're surly. What's the fun of
that anyway?

AGNES:
I guess I'd be better off sitting in front of the TV all
my life.

LOUISE:
Maybe you would be. Gimme that.

AGNES:
No.

LOUISE:
It's mine, gimme it.

AGNES:
Forget it.

LOUISE:
You can't tell me what to do.

AGNES:
Yes I can.

LOUISE:
No you can't.

AGNES:
Just watch me.

THERESA:
Please! Look, Louise, look let's just ... sit down.

LOUISE:
Yeah I'll sit down, in front of my show.

THERESA:
Sit down.

LOUISE:
No.

THERESA:
There's something we have to talk about.

LOUISE:
No. What?

> *THERESA takes out the note LOUISE gave her last night. Pause. LOUISE sits.*

AGNES:
What's that?

THERESA:
It's a note from Mother.

AGNES:
Yes. So? What does it say?

> *THERESA gives AGNES the note. AGNES looks at it for a moment.*

AGNES:
What is it? A 'B'? What's a 'B' for?

THERESA:
Bradley.

AGNES:
Bradley?

THERESA:
Dad.

AGNES:
What about him?

THERESA:
Mother wants us to see him, the three of us.

AGNES:
You're not serious.

THERESA:
She wants us all to make amends.

AGNES:
Make amends? Make amends of what? I'm not
seeing him.

LOUISE:
On *Ryan's Cove* Kara's father came back from living
in France for ten years and she saw him ...

THERESA:
Mother wants us to.

AGNES:
What good will it do her for us to see that bastard?

LOUISE:
—They went to supper at Palmer's—that's the really
nice restaurant ...

THERESA:
She wants to feel that some peace has been made.

AGNES:
It's nothing to do with me ...

LOUISE:
She didn't even know she had a father.

THERESA:
I know it's hard.

AGNES:
It's not hard, it's not hard at all, because it's not going to happen.

LOUISE:
He turned out to be really nice.

AGNES:
Who?

LOUISE:
Kara's father.

AGNES:
I don't know any Kara.

LOUISE:
Kara Ryan.

THERESA:
Let's just talk about it. Or just think about it.

AGNES:
Talk about it all you like, think about it 'til your brain turns blue I don't care. 'B' is right. But it's not 'B' for Bradley. It's 'B' for lousy, rotten, stinking bastard.

AGNES exits.

LOUISE:
They had a really nice time. A nice dinner and all that. Then for about two weeks Kara got nice. Not making evil plans against her mother. Not running around on Justin. But the thing was she got kind of boring then. Until it turned out that her father was just trying to get money out of her to support his

gambling addiction. Then she got bad and interesting again.

AGNES returns with her suitcase and some clothes in her arms.

THERESA:
Where are you going?

AGNES:
Look. I am a grown woman. I have my own life, I make my own decisions. I'm not going to be told who to see or when, I'm not going to be counting my drinks, I am not going to be instructed how to speak, or what to do, or when to do it. It's going to be better for everyone if I just go and stay in a hotel.

THERESA:
Don't be silly.

AGNES:
In a hotel where I can be as "silly" as I like.

THERESA:
Always looking for an excuse.

AGNES:
For what?

LOUISE:
So you can drink without anybody knowing.

AGNES:
I wasn't talking to you. Brat.

THERESA:
To avoid whatever you find unpleasant.

AGNES:
Don't talk to me about avoiding, Saint Theresa. You're the one who's avoiding. Out there in the

bowels of New Brunswick, farming for God. Try living in the world for a week or two and then talk to me about avoiding things.

LOUISE:
Agnes?

AGNES:
No, I'm going. I refuse to stay here.

LOUISE:
Then can I have my clicker back.

> *AGNES realizes she still holds the remote control. She drops it on the table. LOUISE picks it up and exits. THERESA exits to her mother's bedroom. We hear the talk show again from the living room. AGNES stands in the room not sure what to do.*

AGNES:
Fine then. Goodbye.

> *After a moment she exits. Light fades as the talk show continues.*

Scene Three

> *Later that night. THERESA sits up reading. Some thumping off stage. After a few moments AGNES enters with her suitcase. She is very tired and a little drunk. AGNES plops herself down in a chair.*

AGNES:
What are you reading, 'Luke' or 'John'?

THERESA:
Margaret Atwood.

AGNES:

Where's the Mistress of the Air Waves?

THERESA:

Asleep. It's two o'clock.

AGNES:

Why aren't you in bed?

THERESA:

I'm reading.

Silence.

AGNES:

Why doesn't anything ever turn out the way we think it will? Does Miss Margaret Atwood have an answer for that one?

THERESA:

I think for that you better try 'Luke.'

AGNES:

It was like Mother had that thing about Marion Bridge. The way she used to talk about it as if it was some kind of paradise. Everything was better there. And every summer she'd get us all geared up about going and then of course something or other would come up—Dad would be off wherever, or one of us would get sick, or Mother would be in a mood. And then finally, finally we end up going. I was … ten … or twelve. And we were all beside ourselves about the trip. You boiled eggs and we made sandwiches—what was it fourteen miles or something? Guess we didn't get out much back then. And on our way there I remember we were being so good and quiet because we didn't want anything to happen so that we wouldn't get there. But we got to Marion Bridge and what was there? A few houses, a post office, two stores, a church and a dirt road leading down to a beach. Just another town. And what did we do? We sat on the beach, we went for a walk and got chased by a dog who bit me, it started to rain, Mother and Dad fought and we went home early. I don't even think we ate our sandwiches. And that was the end of that. Here's me expecting paradise and it turned out to be just another rotten Sunday afternoon.

THERESA:
Where have you been?

AGNES:
Trying to find a hotel that would take my credit card.

THERESA:
What kind is it?

AGNES:
The over the limit kind.

Silence.

AGNES:
I'm so old and I've got nothing.

THERESA:
You've got your acting.

AGNES:
My acting is turning out to be a very expensive, time consuming and demoralizing hobby.

THERESA:
You've got your friends.

AGNES:
My friends are all alcoholics and drug addicts to whom I owe money.

THERESA:
Whatever.

Silence.

AGNES:
I'm just old and ugly.

THERESA:
Don't forget mean.

AGNES:
Thanks a lot.

THERESA:
I'm mad at you.

AGNES:
Look I'll see her tomorrow, I will, I swear.

THERESA:
It's got nothing to do with me, it's between you and her.

AGNES:
Well well.

THERESA:
I'm mad at you.

AGNES:
I'm getting that drift, yeah.

THERESA:
She's your mother Agnes, do you have any idea what that must feel like?

AGNES:
Yes Theresa I do.

THERESA:
Oh ...

AGNES:
 Whatever.

THERESA:
 I didn't mean to ...

AGNES:
 We talked about her tonight. I saw Sandy.

THERESA:
 And how's Sandy?

AGNES:
 Oh you know. Old. And sad.

THERESA:
 Fat and bald?

AGNES:
 He looks alright. A little plump. Not fat. Not yet
 anyway. I think he got hair implants but he's not
 talking. Charlie sort of hinted at it. He's not half
 bad really, Charlie. But God they're sloppy drunks.
 They're a good pair. One of them is crying while
 the other one's getting sick.

THERESA:
 A tag team

AGNES:
 Ha. Yeah. They can keep it going for hours until
 they get confused and one of them is crying in the
 toilet and the other one is throwing up on your
 shoulder.

THERESA:
 You're bad.

   Silence.

AGNES:

We talked about her a little, Sandy and me. He doesn't know too much—apparently she's not Joan anymore. She's 'Joanie' now. And they moved—all the way up to Cape North. They've got a little craft shop type thing. Sandy went up one day a year or so ago. Sandy says she's got my eyes ... Her name is Joanie and she's got my eyes.

THERESA:

You did the right thing.

AGNES:

No I didn't. I did the wrong thing. I made a big terrible mistake. I should have kept her. I wanted to keep her. But they wouldn't let me. Shipped me off to that bloody convent for six months to keep me out of sight and then when she was born, that was that, she was gone and I was supposed to forget about the whole thing. And the worst of it was they let me hold her before they took her away. I don't know if it was cruelty or stupidity—but they brought her in to me for five minutes and I held her and I felt how right that felt and nothing, nothing has ever felt that right again. The next day Mother came to get me and all the way home in the car all she talked about was the goddamn weather. And that's why I can't go in and see her Theresa—because she's in there dying and because she's dying, I'd have to forgive her for what she did. For letting it happen. And I can't forgive her for that.

THERESA:

You were so young.

AGNES:

So what! So what! I was young but I knew what I wanted. And that's more than I can say about myself right now. I wanted to have a baby. That's what I wanted. You say you had a calling, well I had one too. I mean it's not like I knew that at the time. It's not like I had any big scheme or anything. But when I think about it now I must have known what I was doing. What? You think I was in love with Sandy Deveau? Come on! We had sex once! Once! And let me tell you there's a story.

THERESA:

I'm not sure I want to—

AGNES:

Don't worry I'll save it for my memoirs.

THERESA:

Well you always were an unconventional girl.

AGNES:

Surely wanting to have a child hasn't become unconventional.

THERESA:

Well you could have had children. You could still—

AGNES:

I have a child! And sure yes I thought it would happen again—in some other situation—but it didn't. And I'd be nuts to have a kid now—I've screwed up my life so bad the last thing I need is a kid in it. But she should have known. Mother should have known. And the thing is I think she did know. I wanted that baby and it was the right thing to do. But Mother and the bloody church. No—I won't even blame the church—because it was really just all about what would the neighbours think—all about bloody appearances. And I can't forgive her for that.

THERESA:
>
> You don't have to.

AGNES:

> Oh come on, that's what the whole thing is about, that's why I'm supposed to be here, that's how it works.

THERESA:

> You've been spending too much at the movies Agnes my dear. Just because a person is dying doesn't mean everything suddenly works out— that there's some big resolution. This is real life. Real life's messier than the movies. And death's especially messy. You don't have to forgive her. You just have to love her that's all. And I know you do.

> *AGNES sighs and starts to light a cigarette.*

THERESA:

> Oh Agnes don't. Mother will smell it and be on and on about wanting one.

AGNES:

> She's up?

THERESA:

> Oh yes. She mostly just sleeps though the afternoon. This is pretty much her best time really because she's not due for her pills for another hour and she's not as dopey as she gets.

> *Pause.*

THERESA:

> Why don't you go in? Just say hi.

AGNES:

> I don't know.

THERESA:
I'll leave it to you. I'm going to see if I can catch a little sleep.

THERESA touches AGNES' hair.

THERESA:
A very unconventional girl.

THERESA exits. AGNES sits alone. With resolve she stands and heads toward her mother's room. She stops. She returns to the table and picks up the flowers which still sit there. She moves toward her mother's room. She stops again. She returns to the table and picks up her cigarettes and matches. With flowers and cigarettes in hand she goes to see her mother.

Scene Four

The next day. THERESA sits at the table. She looks through the many post-it notes she has collected. We hear AGNES and LOUISE approaching the house.

LOUISE:
(*off*) Of barbers: Saint Matthew. Of bee keepers: Saint Andrew. Of Bolivia: Our Lady of Capucdana. Of Boy Scouts: Saint George. Of brewers: Saint Luka. Of brides: Saint Nicholas. Of butchers: Saint Anthony the Abbot.

THERESA puts the notes back in her pocket. AGNES and LOUISE enter.

LOUISE:
Of cab drivers: Saint Fiacre. Of Canada: Saint Anne and Saint Joseph. Of canoeists: Saint Raymond. Of

childbirth: Saint Gerard Majella. Of cooks: Saint Martha. Of Cuba: Our Lady of Charity. Of dancers: Saint Vitus.

LOUISE passes through the room.

THERESA:
Where were you two?

LOUISE:
(*as she exits*) At the prayer group. Of dentists: Saint Apollonia. Of desperate situations: Saint Jude. Of doctors: Saint Luke. Of domestic animals: Saint Anthony.

THERESA:
(*to AGNES*) And where were you?

AGNES:
At the prayer group.

THERESA:
What?

AGNES:
Don't get your hopes up. I just wanted to check on what Louise was getting herself into.

THERESA:
I see. And what's the verdict?

AGNES:
I met Dory.

LOUISE re-enters.

LOUISE:
Of Ecuador: The Sacred Heart. Of editors: St Clare. Of emigrants ...

AGNES:
She seemed very nice.

THERESA:

Louise, what are you doing?

LOUISE:

All the Patron Saints in alphabetical order of what they're patron of. Dory's teaching me—she knows every single one. I'm up to 'e' but I can't remember 'emigrants.' Ecuador: Sacred Heart. Editors: Saint Clare. England: St George. But emigrants ...

LOUISE wanders off.

AGNES:

So you must have met Dory then?

THERESA:

Oh yes. At Mass and so on.

AGNES:

She's interesting.

THERESA:

She seems nice enough.

AGNES:

Kind of a little ... butch ... don't you think?

THERESA:

Kind of what?

AGNES:

You know ... kind of ... strong.

THERESA:

Well she runs that farm she's got all by herself.

AGNES:

And the prayer meeting, that's quite something. People are awfully affectionate there. Lots of hugging and hand holding and so on.

THERESA:
What do you mean by that.

AGNES:
Nothing. It's nice.

THERESA:
People get filled with the Spirit. They want to share
their good feeling.

AGNES:
"Filled with the Spirit." Hmm.

LOUISE re-enters.

LOUISE:
Of emigrants is either Saint Patrick or Saint Francis
Xavier Something.

AGNES:
Well she certainly is quite a character.

LOUISE:
Who is?

AGNES:
Dory.

LOUISE:
Dory's great. She don't take nothing from nobody.
And you should see her truck. It's beautiful. But
she's selling it though, because she wants to get a
four-by-four.

AGNES:
(*pointedly to THERESA*) A truck.

LOUISE:
But she's selling it.

AGNES:
Do you ever see Dory outside of the prayer group?

LOUISE:
Mass.

AGNES:
But outside of Church I mean?

LOUISE:
Like where?

AGNES:
I don't know. Like a movie.

LOUISE:
What movie?

AGNES:
Any movie.

THERESA:
Most of them are trash.

AGNES:
Or have her over for dinner.

LOUISE:
What do you mean?

AGNES:
Some evening.

LOUISE:
We don't have dinner in the evening.

AGNES:
I mean supper. And rent a video or something.

LOUISE:
What video?

AGNES:
Any video—some video you want to watch.

LOUISE:
   Oh.

THERESA:
   Most of them are trash.

AGNES:
   It would be nice. Give her a call.

LOUISE:
   What do you mean?

AGNES:
   On the phone!

LOUISE:
   I don't have her number.

AGNES:
   Well you could get it.

LOUISE:
   Oh.

THERESA:
   Louise, go see if Mother touched her lunch at all.

AGNES:
   I'll go.

THERESA:
   Louise you go.

   LOUISE exits somewhat confused.

THERESA:
   What are you up to?

AGNES:
   I'm not up to anything. She doesn't have any
   friends. She should have some friends. She should
   get out more, you said that yourself.

THERESA:
Look, I've got myself all worked up into a state here.

AGNES:
It's no big deal.

THERESA:
Not about that. It's Mother—she's on and on about
this—and look, I don't want to start anything here
and please Agnes don't go getting all dramatic on
me but—Mother keeps on about us going to see
Dad.

AGNES:
Well then maybe we should.

THERESA:
What?

AGNES:
Maybe we should.

THERESA:
You've certainly changed your tune.

AGNES:
I'm in a good mood today. I made a decision about
something. I'm going to take a little drive. Up to
Cape North.

THERESA:
Oh Agnes ...

AGNES:
I just want to see her.

THERESA:
Do you think that's such a good idea?

AGNES:
They have a craft shop. I'm going shopping that's
all. I want to get some ... crafts.

THERESA:
They have craft shops in town.

AGNES:
I just want to see her. When I was sitting up there with Mother last night I realized ... I mean we didn't say much. She wrote a couple of notes. But it was just the being there—there was something in it that was—it was a feeling—or more than that—a truth or—just a knowing—in a way that couldn't be denied. She's my mother and I'm her daughter and whatever happened happened and that's just more—just realer than words or memories or anything else. Do you understand?

THERESA:
She wrote some notes?

AGNES:
I left them on her table I think.

THERESA:
Louise likes to save them.

AGNES:
I'm going to Cape North. I just want to see her.

THERESA:
And you won't say a thing?

AGNES:
Well, I'll say "hi" or "how are you" but I'm not going to say, "Hi, how are you? I'm your mother."

THERESA:
Oh Agnes ...

AGNES:
It's decided. Oh and look, I got this.

AGNES produces a small brass bell.

AGNES:
For Mother when she needs something, just a
little … *(she rings the bell)*

THERESA:
That's nice.

*AGNES heads off toward her mother's room. She
pauses.*

AGNES:
And it's good that we should see Dad. I think it's a
good idea.

AGNES exits. THERESA is alone.

THERESA:
Well I don't know if it is. I don't know if it is at all.

Scene Five

*A few days later. The stage is empty. A bell rings
upstairs. LOUISE crosses though the room and out.
She is wearing a skirt and her hair is wet. THERESA
enters attacking her sweater with a lint brush.
LOUISE re-enters.*

LOUISE:
Are we going or what?

THERESA:
When Agnes gets back we'll go.

LOUISE:
Well when's she getting back?

THERESA:
When she gets here.

LOUISE:
That's not an answer.

THERESA:
Look at you!

LOUISE:
What?

LOUISE plunks herself down in a chair.

THERESA:
You're wearing a skirt!

LOUISE:
So?

THERESA:
You look nice in a skirt.

LOUISE:
How come whenever I wear a skirt everybody goes
"You're wearing a skirt!"?

THERESA:
Well you hardly every wear a skirt.

LOUISE:
'Cause everybody's always talking about it when I
do.

THERESA:
It's nice you're wearing a skirt.

LOUISE:
If we ever get to go.

THERESA:
Aren't you missing your show?

LOUISE:
Which one?

THERESA:
Ryan's Thingy.

LOUISE:
Ryan's Cove. Ah it's getting so dumb. Nothing ever happens on it.

THERESA:
Seems to me like lots happens on it.

LOUISE:
But nothing ever ends up anywhere. It's so not realistic. Like the identical cousin thing. Or that time Kara was a werewolf but Justin just ended up dreaming it. A two week dream! Come on! And now they've got aliens landing in the cove.

The bell rings upstairs.

LOUISE:
I'll go. I've gotta do something I'm going nuts waiting. Should I put on pants?

THERESA:
No. You look nice.

The bell rings upstairs. LOUISE exits. THERESA is alone.

After a moment she goes into the living room. She turns on the television and we hear the following dialogue.

JUSTIN: "But Kara don't you understand he's an alien"

KARA: "Don't be silly Justin, no alien could make love to a woman like he does."

JUSTIN: "What! Kara! What are you saying?"

KARA: "I'm saying … read my lips Justin: I'm
        saying I feel like a woman for the first time
        in my life."

*AGNES enters in a state. She circles the room once and
then exits. THERESA turns off the television and
re-enters. AGNES re-enters with a drink.*

THERESA:
You're back.

AGNES drinks it down in one shot.

THERESA:
Well what happened?

*AGNES exits. After a moment she returns with another
drink.*

THERESA:
Agnes...

AGNES:
It's alright it's my first of the day.

THERESA:
Second.

AGNES:
That was my first.

She downs the shot.

AGNES:
That was my second.

THERESA:
What happened?

AGNES:
I saw her.

THERESA:
> You saw her.

AGNES:
> I saw her. I talked to her.

THERESA:
> You told her?

AGNES:
> No. But I talked to her.

THERESA:
> What was she like?

> *During the following speech AGNES exits and returns with another drink which she sips throughout.*

AGNES:
> She's beautiful. She's just … She's built sort of like Louise and she's got your face and my hair—but Mother's eyes, not mine at all. And thank God I think she got off lucky because I couldn't see a trace of Sandy in her.

THERESA:
> What happened?

AGNES:
> Well I went into the store. Her and her … God I find it hard to say … Her and her mother have this craft store. It's nice, you know, simple. She's trying to get her high school—she never got her high school—because she wants to go to technical school in Halifax for hairdressing or design, she can't decide because her boyfriend—oh my God she's got a boyfriend—because her boyfriend, Steve I think it was, has got a line on a job in Halifax. And she hates Cape North but she loves Jane Eyre.

THERESA:

  Jane Eyre?

AGNES:

  She's reading it for her English. And she loves to
  laugh, but she hates Cape North and she's
  desperate to get out.

THERESA:

  How did you find all this out?

AGNES:

  I talked to her! She was just desperate to talk to
  somebody … I met the mother.

THERESA:

  You did?

AGNES:

  I don't like her. Cold. Not at all friendly. Nothing
  like Joanie. Joanie. Oh my God.

THERESA:

  What do you mean cold?

AGNES:

  Nothing like Joanie. Cold. Just cold. They don't get
  along, you can tell.

THERESA:

  Agnes.

AGNES:

  What? Nothing! I'm just saying what I saw.

THERESA:

  What are you thinking?

AGNES:

  I'm not thinking anything. Anyway we'll see what
  happens Wednesday.

THERESA:
What's Wednesday?

AGNES:
My pottery class.

THERESA:
Pottery class?

AGNES:
The mother … Chrissy, she teaches a pottery class at
the store a few times a week and Joanie helps out
with it.

THERESA:
Agnes.

AGNES:
We'll just get to be friendly that's all. And from what
I can tell she sure needs a friend.

THERESA:
It's not a good idea.

AGNES:
It's fine. It's nothing. And I always liked pottery.

THERESA:
Since when?

AGNES:
Since lately.

>   *LOUISE enters.*

LOUISE:
It's about time! Let's go.

AGNES:
Go where?

THERESA:
We're having dinner at Dad's.

AGNES:

Oh no, I totally forgot.

LOUISE:

What do you mean?

THERESA:

Are you alright for it? Do you want to postpone it?

LOUISE:

Noooo!

AGNES:

No, fine, no, let's get it all done in a day that's the way to do it. What time did we say we'd be there?

LOUISE:

Long ago!

THERESA:

Now.

AGNES:

Alright. Good. Here's the deal: we are going to go out as a happy united little family to our father's house and have dinner with him and his ... little Lolita.

LOUISE:

Connie.

AGNES:

Whatever. We will eat our meal, I will not drink two bottles of wine and attack him with a butter knife, exactly ninety minutes after we arrive we will leave, and then we will come home and tell Mother we had a wonderful time and that will be the end of it.

LOUISE:

What if we do have a wonderful time?

AGNES:
And what if the NDP ran the world?

THERESA:
I'm just not sure about leaving Mother.

AGNES:
She said she'll be fine and we'll be back in two hours. Did she take her pills?

LOUISE:
I just gave them to her.

THERESA:
I don't know.

AGNES:
Mother wants us all to go, that's part of the deal.

THERESA:
It's not so much him I mind seeing as Lolita.

LOUISE:
Connie.

THERESA:
Whatever.

AGNES:
So while I'm at him with the butter knife you can get her with the fork.

LOUISE:
Are we going or what?

AGNES:
(*finishing her drink*) Come on troops! To the front line!

THERESA:
Alright.

AGNES:
Oh my!

LOUISE:
What?

AGNES:
You're wearing a skirt!

LOUISE:
I'm changing!

AGNES:
No you look great, come on.

The three women start out. They talk as they exit.

AGNES:
Oh what's up with the aliens?

LOUISE:
I don't know that show's getting so dumb.

AGNES:
I like that blonde alien guy.

THERESA:
Apparently so does Kara.

AGNES:
How do you know?

THERESA:
Oh, I just caught a bit of it looking for the news.

Scene Six

Later that evening THERESA, AGNES and LOUISE enter.

THERESA:
I can't believe it! I just can't believe it! It's scandalous! It's criminal! It's just … And the go of her! The queen of the castle! And the look of him!

LOUISE:
That was so no fun.

THERESA:
So no fun! No fun indeed! Infuriating more like it!

LOUISE:
I'll go see Mother.

LOUISE exits.

THERESA:
I almost had a drink I swear. I was that angry.

AGNES:
Don't get yourself in a state.

AGNES exits.

THERESA:
Get?! Get?! I'm gone! I'm there! And it's not a state either it's bigger, it's a province! No it's bigger, it's a territory! It's a country! It's a continent!

AGNES returns with two shots. She offers one to THERESA.

THERESA:
Don't be ridiculous.

AGNES pours THERESA's shot into her glass.

AGNES:

At least it's over with.

THERESA:

I'm beside myself! On both sides. This one here and this one here and they're both angrier than I am! I can't believe how you can be so calm.

AGNES:

You're worked up enough for all of us. Anyway she's just another one of those Deena Jessome types.

THERESA:

Who?

AGNES:

You know Deena Jessome. From school. Dougie's sister.

THERESA:

Oh yes well she was ... yes, but she was ...

AGNES:

A slut.

THERESA:

Agnes.

AGNES:

She was. She went out with the whole hockey team.

THERESA:

Well she had a lot of dates.

AGNES:

The whole hockey team. At the same time.

THERESA:

But I liked Deena Jessome. At least she was what she was and was honest about it. Not like this rig. Oh dear! I've got to ... I don't know what I've got to do. I should have a cup of tea. No that'll just wind me

up more. Perhaps I should just head to bed. But
there's not much chance of me sleeping bolt
upright and raving is there.

AGNES:

It wasn't so bad.

THERESA:

It wasn't so bad? Her acting the happy little
housewife. She didn't even know how to operate the
stove! What does she feed him? You couldn't even
eat the turkey, it was that tough. And I don't know
who would have the nerve to call those grey things
potatoes. And what was she wearing?

AGNES:

A halter top.

THERESA:

A little piece of nothing and some string. And
prancing around like some kind of teenager. And
that house! Who needs five bedrooms? And that
awful little dog. "Baby"! What kind of name is that
for a dog? And Dad never liked dogs. And she's
getting two more, did you hear her when she said
she was getting two more? And a dishwasher! She
can't use the stove what's she going to do with a
dishwasher? Unless she's going to use it to wash the
dogs.

AGNES:

I feel sorry for her.

THERESA:

Sorry for her? And who was the fella in the
basement!?

AGNES:

Her cousin she said.

THERESA:
Her cousin? I'm sure!

AGNES:
Well well what are you thinking—perhaps you've been spending a bit too much time with *Ryan's Cove.*

THERESA:
Come on! What's she got her cousin there for?

AGNES:
You heard her, he's just there to help build the pool.

THERESA:
The pool! The pool! What in the name of all that is good and holy does Dad need with a pool? He can't even make it up and down the stairs by himself.

AGNES:
Well it was his choice to be with her.

THERESA:
And her calling him 'Daddy.' If that's not enough to turn you off your meal.

AGNES:
Well you found the turkey tough anyway.

THERESA:
And what a mess he's in.

AGNES:
(*laughing*) "Pass the binoculars."

THERESA:
What?

AGNES:
"Pass the binoculars."

THERESA:
Oh now I know.

AGNES:
(*laughing*) "Pass the binoculars."

THERESA:
Oh I know, don't laugh.

AGNES:
But you've got to hand it to her though, cool as a cucumber. He says "Pass the binoculars" and she just passes him a bun like nothing's wrong.

THERESA:
She made a joke of it.

AGNES:
Well what else are you going to do?

THERESA:
And he couldn't even remember Louise's name.

AGNES:
It can't be much of a life for her though.

THERESA:
Oh come on, she's got poor old Dad's pension and the mansion on the hill and the cousin in the basement.

AGNES:
And when the phone rang and he says, "Get the tub."

THERESA:
(*laughing*) Oh no, I know, don't laugh.

AGNES:
But he was pretty close though with the buns. I mean they were hard as binoculars.

THERESA:

(*laughing*) Stop.

AGNES:

(*laughing*) "Pass the binoculars and get the tub."

THERESA:

(*laughing*) The binoculars were so, though they should have had a good soak in the phone before she served them!

AGNES:

Poor Connie.

THERESA:

Serves her right.

LOUISE enters.

AGNES:

How's Mother? Louise? How's Mother?

THERESA:

Louise? How's Mother?

LOUISE:

She wouldn't wake up. I tried but she wouldn't.

THERESA:

Oh good lord ...

THERESA exits to her Mother's room. AGNES rises to exit.

LOUISE:

I tried to wake her up but she wouldn't. And I leaned down and I said to her, "Mother?" I said. And I was going to tell her about being at Dad's but I was going to make it sound nice and that. And I said "Mother?" But she wouldn't wake up. So I touched her arm. I touched her arm and I could tell that she wasn't there. She was there but she wasn't there. Part of her was there but the part of her that was there wasn't her. She's up there but she's not. Where is she?

THERESA re-enters, upset.

THERESA:
Agnes. She's gone.

AGNES:
Oh God. Oh God.

THERESA:
She was all alone.

AGNES:
She was all alone.

LOUISE:
She had this in her hand.

LOUISE holds up a note.

THERESA:
She was all alone.

The women do not touch. They remain separate as the light fades.

LOUISE:
It's a heart.

AGNES:
She was alone.

LOUISE:
A little heart.

End of Act One.

ACT TWO

Scene One

We hear a young girl singing the hymn "Be Not Afraid" in a strong, clear voice. Light up on THERESA alone. She addresses the audience.

THERESA:

On the farm where I live we have animals—two cows and some chickens, a rooster, a tired old horse called Matilda and more cats than we can keep track of. And from the animals we get eggs, and milk, and lots of kittens. Now we've got a tractor but when I first got there about ten years ago we used Matilda to haul the tiller—the Sisters there believe that it's best to use living things to make living things. Of the earth, for the earth, from the earth. And some of them say that the vegetables were better—bigger and tastier—when Matilda did the work, but most of them have come around to seeing a tractor as a kind of a living thing: you've got to clean it and you've got to feed it and it has a real temperament. Farming is wonderful: getting your hands down there in the beautiful dirt. When you're working in it up to your elbows it starts to feel like liquid, thick dark liquid, like the blood of the earth. And that's really all I've got: the farm, the animals, the earth. And my faith. But lately I've been wondering if I'm there more for the farm than the faith. But one thing about the faith I know is right is the idea of owning nothing, having nothing but each day. Although since I've been back home … I've never been one for collecting anything but there's something about these:

She takes a large collection of the yellow post-it notes from her pocket.

Mother's notes. They're so beautiful. At first just a bunch of marks and squiggles but once you understand it it's as big and wonderful as any language. I let on they were for Louise but really they're my special connection to Mother. We always got on, me and Mother, but in that way that there's not too much to say. With Agnes there was turmoil and tumult and Louise always had her odd ways, but I was the one in the middle. The good one, the peacemaker. There was never too much need for drama between Mother and me. There was her drinking—but I wasn't really supposed to know about that—and I guess I chose not to know. And once Dad left well it didn't seem like she had much more than her few drinks every night and her books. She always had a book on the go. But the funny thing is … I remember one day when I was little she was reading a book and she had that sort of dreamy look on her face that she got when she read and I watched her—she didn't know I was there but I watched her for a long time, maybe as long as fifteen minutes—and in all that time she never turned a page and I realized that she just used the book as a kind of a decoy. A trick she used to escape into her own world. Wherever that was.

And I guess the distance between her and her secret world was the distance I felt between Mother and me. But all these, these little notes, this language, these make me feel like I understand something. It was a lovely service. Father Dave spoke beautifully. Mother's favourite hymns. Agnes read from 'John.' Mother loved 'John' and Agnes was always so good to read. It didn't take us long to realize that Mother had arranged for the circumstances of her departure. She wanted to be alone. It was her final choice. No resolution. She left this world as she wished to, on her own. In her secret world. And there's a certain beauty in that I suppose. And a strangeness too. But people are strange. Never what you expect. Not like the farm. From the soil you can expect the vegetables and from the animals you can expect the milk and the eggs and the kittens. But from people ... Best not to have expectations and to keep your plans flexible.

THERESA gathers up the notes.

Today I went to look at the stone. It's lovely. A praying hands on one side and an open book on the other. I find it particularly fitting that the book is marble. The pages will never turn. But lovely work, really lovely.

The light shifts and THERESA turns into the scene. She speaks to AGNES who is taking off her coat after having just entered. AGNES paces back and forth.

THERESA:
That fellow takes such care. Not like you know, all prefab or whatever you get today. Real time. Real care. What are you all wound up about?

79

AGNES:
Nothing nothing.

THERESA:
You know Louise still hasn't come out of her room today. Dory called again but she wouldn't even take the phone. Might be partly to do with Mother's insurance cheque coming. Got her down all over again. I told her maybe we could use it toward a new car. I though that might cheer her up but no doing. Might be nice if you spent some time with her. What's the matter? How was your pottery class?

AGNES:
Oh dear.

THERESA:
What is it?

AGNES:
She's a monster Theresa.

THERESA:
Who is?

AGNES:
The mother. Chrissy. She's awful with her.

THERESA:
How?

AGNES:
See the story is—which I just got—see after Chrissy got Joanie her husband took off and she got together with this other guy and they ended up having two of their own and well I guess the sun just shines right out of their … You know. And Joanie she just can't do a thing right.

THERESA:
Where are you getting this?

AGNES:
From Joanie.

THERESA:
Well she's young, you know she's going to say—

AGNES:
I've seen it! I've got eyes. I see how she treats her.
She's not good with her. And she's wild Joanie is.
She dropped her summer course and apparently
she's in the bar every night with that Steve—and I
don't like the look of him. Trouble in a cap that
one is. See she has no proper guidance.

THERESA:
Agnes.

AGNES:
What?

THERESA:
Where's this headed?

AGNES:
Nowhere. I don't know. Nowhere. She needs help.

THERESA:
She's not a child.

AGNES:
No but she is in a way. She's had no guidance.

THERESA:
You're probably not getting the whole story.

AGNES:
I can feel it Theresa. In my gut. It's a troubled
situation.

THERESA:
Yes well we've got situations here.

AGNES:
She's my daughter.

THERESA:
But she doesn't know that.

AGNES:
But if she did—

LOUISE:
Agnes. Look. I understand your concern and so on but don't you think you should spend a little time with Louise? She's going through something here.

AGNES:
Well we're all going through something.

THERESA:
Yes but you've lost people before, I've lost people, Louise hasn't. I try to talk to her but she doesn't hear me, it's you she needs right now.

AGNES:
I've spent time with her.

THERESA:
How many times have you been to Cape North since the funeral? Four? Five?

AGNES:
Something like—

THERESA:
Six? You have barely spent a proper day here and when you are here all you're thinking about is … well, whatever scheme it is you're hatching.

AGNES:
I'm not hatching anything.

THERESA:

Ha!

AGNES rises and moves to exit.

AGNES:

Get off my back.

THERESA:

Yes that's it, go have a few drinks that'll sort things
out fine.

AGNES:

What?

THERESA:

Go on, just like always.

AGNES:

Listen sister darling, I haven't had a drink since the
funeral. What you've got here is the real me, one
hundred percent full out Agnes MacKeigan,
unbuzzed and unsedated. The creature in nature as
it was born, all for your viewing and listening
pleasure. But if you're trying to drive me to it you're
doing a hell of a job.

THERESA:

You're still drunk though. Maybe not with booze
but now it's with that girl. You just traded one for
the other. All your thoughts with her when they
should be with your family.

AGNES:

Joanie is my family.

THERESA:

We're your family. Louise is your family. And it's not
just Mother either. That Dory's calling here three or

four times a day. Something's going on and there's no denying you've had a hand in it.

AGNES:
What the hell do you mean by that?

THERESA:
I mean what I mean.

AGNES:
Which is what?

THERESA:
"Why don't you have her for supper?" "Go see a movie." "Rent a video." The sly little grin—all smart and worldly.

AGNES:
There's no harm in her having a friend. I didn't know she'd become cloistered.

THERESA:
I wasn't born yesterday. I hear what people say about Dory Ferguson.

AGNES:
Which is what?

THERESA:
Which is ... whatever.

AGNES:
Say it. What?

LOUISE appears suddenly.

THERESA:
Well if it isn't sleeping beauty.

LOUISE:
I wasn't sleeping. What are you talking about?

THERESA:
Oh you know.

AGNES:
Nothing.

LOUISE:
Nothing?

AGNES:
No nothing.

LOUISE:
Your mouths were moving and words were coming out but you were talking about nothing?

AGNES:
Nothing really.

LOUISE:
Nothing really for me to know. Just like everything.

THERESA:
What everything?

LOUISE:
Everything everything. Like when Dad left and everybody said he was on a trip. Like Mother not even saying goodbye. Like everything. Like Marion Bridge that time.

THERESA:
What time.

LOUISE:
That time you all went and I didn't.

AGNES:
We only went the one time. You were there.

LOUISE:

Was not. It was supposed to be all special and that and then I had the chicken pox and Mother said we'd wait till next week but Dad said no you were going anyway and you two made egg salad sandwiches and went off without me.

AGNES:

You weren't there?

LOUISE:

That's what I'm saying and I had to stay here with Deena Jessome babysitting me with all them boys around who I hated and then you all came back and you gave me the egg salad sandwiches to make me feel better but I couldn't eat them because they were all sat on, and I was sick right, I couldn't eat them anyway even if they weren't sat on, and I ended up getting sicker on top of the chicken pox because Deena Jessome's boyfriends kept me locked out of the house all afternoon and it rained.

AGNES:

Where's this coming from?

LOUISE:

I never get to be part of nothing.

AGNES:

We can go to Marion Bridge. We can go tomorrow.

LOUISE:

No! No it's too late. Dad's gone and Mother's gone and I never get to be part of anything. Always always 'cause I'm strange or something. (*to AGNES*) And you're gone all the time. Where do you go all the time?

AGNES:
   Nowhere.

LOUISE:
   Lie! Tell me.

AGNES:
   Nowhere.

LOUISE:
   Tell me!

AGNES:
   No.

LOUISE:
   See! See!

   LOUISE exits.

AGNES:
   Christ.

THERESA:
   See?

AGNES:
   Get. Off. My. Back.

THERESA:
   Finish cleaning your own house before you start on
   the neighbours.

AGNES:
   That would be 'Luke' would it? Or 'Acts'?

THERESA:
   Such a comedian.

   THERESA picks up the car keys and moves to exit.

AGNES:
   Where are you going?

THERESA:
Nowhere.

She moves to exit and then stops.

THERESA:
Will you be here when I get back?

AGNES:
Not if you're lucky.

THERESA:
So be it.

THERESA exits.

AGNES paces back and forth in the kitchen. She goes to exit. She stops. She sits. She rises and moves to exit. She stops. She plunks herself down in the chair. She growls in frustration. She drops her head to her chest. She sits up. She sighs.

After a moment:

AGNES:
Louise!!

Scene Two

Later that evening. AGNES and LOUISE sit at the table playing cards.

AGNES:
(*placing a card on the pile*) Oh I hate to do it but I've got nothing but that.

LOUISE moves to draw from the deck.

AGNES:
Aren't you going for hearts?

LOUISE:
Yeah.

AGNES:
Well I just threw out the Queen.

LOUISE:
Oh yeah.

LOUISE picks up AGNES' discard.

LOUISE:
Rummy.

AGNES:
Oh you won again!

LOUISE:
(*unenthusiastically*) Hooray.

AGNES:
Another hand?

LOUISE:
I don't care.

AGNES:
Your deal.

LOUISE:
Go ahead.

AGNES shuffles and deals. They play throughout.

AGNES:
So how are you?

LOUISE:
How come you keep asking me that?

AGNES:
Because you haven't answered.

LOUISE:
Fine.

AGNES:
What are you thinking about?

LOUISE:
I don't know.

AGNES:
Mother?

LOUISE:
I guess.

AGNES:
What about her?

LOUISE:
I don't know.

Silence.

LOUISE:
Do you think she's in heaven?

AGNES:
Of course she is.

LOUISE:
Stuart from the prayer group says you have to spend
until the end of time in limbo even if you were
really really good and then when the world ends
pretty much only saints get into heaven.

AGNES:
Yes but it's different for mothers.

LOUISE:
Is it?

AGNES:
Oh yeah.

LOUISE:
Oh. So she's in heaven.

AGNES:
Playing cards with Saint Peter.

LOUISE:
She liked Saint Jude.

AGNES:
They're playing 45's and Saint Jude is her partner.

LOUISE:
And what about us.

AGNES:
What about us?

LOUISE:
Will we go to heaven?

AGNES:
Well by that time Mother will be in with all of the
big wigs up there and she'll have the pull so I don't
see why not.

Silence.

LOUISE:
How old is she, like in heaven?

AGNES:
What do you mean?

LOUISE:
Well is she like old as she was when she died and
kind of sick and that?

AGNES:
In heaven you get to choose whatever age you want
to be.

LOUISE:
Really?

AGNES:
Uh huh.

LOUISE:
So she could choose like eleven or eighteen or six
or something?

AGNES:
Whatever she wanted to be.

LOUISE:
So say she chose eleven.

AGNES:
Uh huh.

LOUISE:
So if she chose eleven or six or something or some
age she was before we knew her how would we
recognize her when we got there?

AGNES:
Well ...

LOUISE:
Maybe what we could do is go through all the
pictures of her that we've got and put them all in
order of how old she was and then we'd remember
what she looked like from when she was a baby.

AGNES:
I think that's an excellent idea.

LOUISE:
Your go.

AGNES:
Sorry?

LOUISE:
I threw you go.

AGNES:
Oh right.

AGNES picks a card. They continue to play.

Silence.

AGNES:
And so how else are you?

LOUISE:
What do you mean?

AGNES:
I mean is there anything else on your mind?

LOUISE:
I don't know. Like what?

AGNES:
Like I don't know. Like something you're feeling?

LOUISE:
Feeling how?

AGNES:
Just feeling. Or thinking about.

LOUISE:
I don't know.

AGNES:
Because sometimes it helps to talk about things.

LOUISE:
You talk.

AGNES:
   I am talking.

LOUISE:
   No you're not, you're asking questions.

   Silence.

LOUISE:
   It's your go.

AGNES:
   Louise? What's bothering you? I mean really.

LOUISE:
   I don't know. Nothing. Or I don't know. Something,
   I guess. It's your go.

AGNES:
   I think I might know what it is.

LOUISE:
   Yeah?

AGNES:
   I think so.

LOUISE:
   It's your go.

   AGNES continues to play.

AGNES:
   Like something about someone?

LOUISE:
   I don't know.

AGNES:
   Like something about Dory?

LOUISE:
   I don't know. Yeah.

AGNES:
Look honey, nobody can tell you the right thing to think or the right thing to do but you know inside what's right. If you feel something or want something then that's okay—and you can talk about anything you want to talk about with me.

    Silence.

AGNES:
Or if it's something to do with Dory then you can talk to her about it. But you shouldn't keep things inside you should talk about them. And I just want you to know—Louise listen to me—I just want you to know that whatever you feel it's okay. Nobody can tell you what's right for you. You know inside. You do what you need to do.

LOUISE:
Yeah?

AGNES:
Yeah.

LOUISE:
Okay.

AGNES:
Are you okay?

LOUISE:
Yeah. Are you okay?

AGNES:
Of course I'm okay.

    AGNES gives LOUISE a hug.

LOUISE:
Yikes! What's that for?

AGNES:
> Because I love you.

LOUISE:
> Get out of here. It's your go.

> *AGNES discards. LOUISE picks it up.*

LOUISE:
> Rummy.

AGNES:
> How did you do that?

> *LOUISE shuffles the cards.*

LOUISE:
> You should talk less and watch your cards more.

Scene Three

A week later. The stage is empty. We hear Ryan's Cove dialogue in the living room.

KARA: "Oh Justin I'm sorry. I didn't mean to hurt you.

JUSTIN: "I know you didn't my love I know."

THERESA backs onto the stage from the living room. She is holding the remote control, mesmerized by the television.

KARA: "You know what I'd like to do my darling?"

JUSTIN: "What sweet one?"

KARA: "Let's go for a lovely drive in the country."

THERESA:
No no don't do it! It's s trick!

JUSTIN: "That would be wonderful."

THERESA:
No no she's in with the aliens! Don't do it!

KARA: "Yes absolutely wonderful."

THERESA:
That Kara she's just pure evil.

AGNES enters. THERESA turns off the television and sticks the remote in her pocket.

THERESA:
Hello.

AGNES:
Yes. Hi. Where's Louise?

THERESA:
Out to the prayer group.

AGNES:
That's good. She seems better eh?

THERESA:
Yes. It's good you've been spending some time with her.

AGNES:
Yes.

THERESA:
And managing to keep up your pottery classes at the same time.

AGNES:
Mmmm.

THERESA:
And how's that going?

AGNES:
Well you know I'm not really too much for getting my hands dirty and it's hard to do that pottery stuff without making quite a mess. You know. Um.

THERESA:
Something on your mind?

AGNES:
Oh nothing.

THERESA:
Nothing is it?

AGNES:
Oh no not really too much not really no.

THERESA:
I see. (*she heads to exit*) Well I'm just going to go for a—

AGNES:
Well no, well actually ...

THERESA:
Actually?

AGNES:
Actually. (*she clears her throat*) I had a lovely day.

THERESA:
Did you?

AGNES:
Yes. I uh ... I skipped class today and Joanie and I spent the afternoon together.

THERESA:
Did you? That's nice I guess.

AGNES:
Yes it was. And um ...

THERESA:
Mm hm?

AGNES:
Well.

THERESA:
Well.

AGNES:
There's a little ... thing.

THERESA:
A thing.

AGNES:
Uh huh.

THERESA:
What kind of thing?

AGNES:
A thing. A sort of a wrinkle.

THERESA:
A wrinkle.

AGNES:
An interesting development.

THERESA:
Interesting?

AGNES:
I guess you could call it I suppose if you wanted to a bit of a problem.

THERESA:

A problem.

AGNES:

But perhaps if you wanted to you might see it not so
much as a problem as an opportunity.

THERESA:

Agnes do you think we might cut to the chase here?

AGNES:

(*she clears her throat*) It seems that things have
reached a head between Joanie and the mother.

THERESA:

Chrissy.

AGNES:

Chrissy yes.

THERESA:

Um hm.

AGNES:

They had words and Chrissy put her out of the
house and Joanie has nowhere to stay—the last
couple of days she's been staying with a girl she
knows—this tiny tiny little place, barely room for
one really, not even a proper kitchen.

THERESA:

Agnes?

AGNES:

And I just thought that it might be a good idea that
she come and stay here for awhile.

THERESA:

With us?

AGNES:

Well you'll be leaving soon anyway.

THERESA:
I'm in no rush, they said I could take the time I
need. And frankly I could use a bit of time.

AGNES:
Well that's fine, there's lots of room for all of us.

THERESA:
And what about you? What about Toronto?

AGNES:
There's nothing there for me—and anyway
Toronto's not going anywhere, I can always go back.

THERESA:
Did you tell her?

AGNES:
What?

THERESA:
Who you were?

AGNES:
No no. Not yet. Maybe later. When things settle
down a bit.

THERESA:
I just don't think it's a very good idea.

AGNES:
Why not?

THERESA:
We could— Maybe we could scrape up a bit of
money to help her out but I don't think moving in
here is the answer.

AGNES:
Why not?

THERESA:

And she's not a child. She can get a job—get her own place.

AGNES:

She's family.

THERESA:

You're doing it again Agnes.

AGNES:

Look, this is a chance for me— This is an opportunity for me to set some things right. Mistakes were made in the past—and I'm not blaming anyone anymore, there's no point in that. I'm just saying that this is a chance to make something good happen.

THERESA:

No.

AGNES:

Why not?

THERESA:

No.

AGNES:

Don't say no, say maybe.

THERESA:

No.

AGNES:

I just need you to say that you think it's a good idea. And now that you're going to be here well you'll be part of it too.

THERESA:

No Agnes.

AGNES:

Why not?

THERESA:

Agnes, we've got Louise up to who knows what and
you're a tantrum away from a two day binge and I'm
spending more time with Justin and Kara than in
church.

AGNES:

I haven't had a drink in a month!

THERESA:

Yes and how many times have you done that before
and how many times have you gone back?

AGNES:

Thanks for your support.

THERESA:

No ... Look ... You said yourself your life was too
messed up to think about having a child in it.

AGNES:

Yes, my life as it was! But now it's changing!

THERESA:

Oh yes.

AGNES:

You don't think I can change?

THERESA:

Like the weather.

AGNES:

Look, she wouldn't be in my life as my child, she
just thinks she's my friend you see, so there
wouldn't be any of those sort of complications. See?

THERESA:

I thought she was family.

AGNES:
Family to us, friend to her.

THERESA:
Agnes, get your story straight.

AGNES:
That's what I'm trying to do. I'm just trying to make some kind of story. I've spent so long trying to tell other people's stories. Telling stories in dirty basements with people who think crazy means brilliant and brilliant means poor. Telling stories I don't even understand. I want my story. And I made a mess of it—I let other people make a mess of it, now I can fix it.

THERESA:
Dear we've none of us got a clue where we're headed—

AGNES:
It could be great. We'll all figure things out together.

THERESA:
Yes, a perfect fairy tale.

AGNES:
It's the right thing to do.

THERESA:
You don't even know this girl.

AGNES:
I do.

THERESA:
And how would you explain her to Louise?

AGNES:
Louise knows a lot more than you think.

THERESA:
No.

AGNES:
Mother would want it.

THERESA:
Oh come on.

AGNES:
She would. If she were upstairs right now I'd go up and tell her and she'd get out her notes and draw a little heart.

THERESA:
This is Cape Breton Agnes, not Hollywood.

AGNES:
It'll be great.

THERESA:
I'm saying no. Not here. Not now.

AGNES:
Yes.

THERESA:
For once in your life would you stop thinking of yourself Agnes?

AGNES:
It is her I'm thinking of. She's got no one. She's scared. Chrissy she won't have anything to do with her and Steve the boyfriend well he's turned out to be the arse I expected—Theresa she's got no one.

THERESA:
Oh stop it. That poor girl has nothing to do with it, you're only concerned about yourself.

AGNES:
How can you say that?

THERESA:
Because I know.

AGNES:
You think you always know, you think you've got it all worked out. Holy Saint Theresa all giving and kind but really you just don't want anyone else to have a life. Not me not Louise. You don't want anyone else to have a life because you don't have one. That's why you're such a bitch.

THERESA:
Oh that's lovely.

AGNES:
Well. You are.

THERESA:
You have no idea about me Agnes, you just have no idea. You think it's all so easy for me but it's not— it's not. This is a life I have—a big life. I'd like to see you try being a nun. People say awful things—they think worse things. And I have a heart you know—I didn't give my heart up when I took my vows. And yes indeed I do live in the world. In this big old awful sick mess of a world. And my heart is filled with questions. Filled. Every time I look around at the world. And when I do look at it what I see is— No, what I *don't* see is God. You've got children killing children and half the world on drugs and the other half starving and people just letting it happen. Where's God in that? And I'm supposed to believe God is everywhere, in everything, in everyone—but sometimes I just don't see him. Imagine how that makes me feel—just as a person— as a person who made a decision and a promise to believe—to see God everywhere. But where is he? Every day—every minute of every day I have to ask

that question because of the choices I've made. And you don't think sometimes I don't just feel like a fool? But I've got to keep believing and I've got to keep loving and giving and helping. But it's all such a mess and I don't know what to do about it. I don't know how to make things right. I don't know how I got here. There's no room Agnes ... I have no room for anyone else ...

THERESA weeps. AGNES comforts her.

Scene Four

LOUISE addresses the audience.

LOUISE:
On the highway and driving, the radio on a really good song. I won't say what the song is 'cause you say one song and somebody hates that song—some people like country and some people like heavy rock some people like no singing, so just say the song is your favourite song. Favourite song, on the highway, driving. Nothing ahead of you, nothing in your rear-view mirror. And the day say, say it's the day. Daytime driving is one thing, nighttime driving that's something else. Nighttime driving, that's heading into yourself but daytime driving is heading out into the world, and here we're talking about heading out out out into the whole world. So it's daytime, summertime, say about six o'clock, and say you're heading east so that the sun's right behind you—and everything all around you is that kind of orange kind of yellow kind of golden kind of colour. And you're in your machine—your car, or

your truck or your hatchback or whatever it is you've got—and there's a warm wind, the window down, and what you got around you is trees and fields and hills and stuff, and what you got ahead of you is a long long line of road, and what you got under you is this machine. Then there's one thing you shouldn't be doing and one thing you should be. The thing you shouldn't be doing is to have a picture in your head of where you're going, people do that—the whole time they're driving they're just imagining the place they're going so that they're not really driving they're really just trying to get somewhere. So you shouldn't have a place in your head. Maybe you shouldn't even know where you're going, you'll only know where it is when you get there. That would be best. And the thing you should be doing is staying really really still. Say you got your arm out the window like this and your hand on the wheel like this and your eyes on the road with your head like this. And you just stay like that, really really still. Of course you're steering a little bit right, just a little bit, just like this. And after awhile if you're not thinking about getting somewhere and you're being really really still, then it's not like you're steering the machine on the road, it's like the road is steering the machine and then it's like you're steering the road and then it's like the road is coming in through the front of the machine and moving right through your body and shooting out the back, it's like the fields and the trees and the hills are these green lines in the golden light all around you and you are the machine you're in and you are the road under you and you are the wind and the air and the light and the music and the empty mirror and it is all moving so quickly and at the same time staying so still …

moving, still, moving, still, both exactly perfectly, moving, still, both at the same time, and everything is you and you are everything.

You might think that'd be strange to think that way but that's okay because people think I'm strange anyway. And maybe I am some ways. I was thinking it might be 'cause I was the only one of the three of us not named for a saint. There's no Saint Louise. And I know 'cause I've been through them all. I haven't got them memorized yet but I'm working on it. But for sure there's no Saint Louise. Maybe there could be someday though. Saint Louise of the Highway. Strange. But see for me it's like everybody's strange, it's just that some people show it more than other people do. I suppose some people would say it's strange for me to be standing here talking to you.

Scene Five

A few days later. AGNES is on her hands and knees scrubbing the floor. LOUISE enters.

LOUISE:
What are you doing?

AGNES:
I'm writing a biography of Winston Churchill.

LOUISE:
Huh?

AGNES:
Louise, what does it look like I'm doing?

LOUISE:
Like you're scrubbing the floor?

AGNES:
Brava.

LOUISE:
Huh?

AGNES:
Yes. I am scrubbing the floor.

LOUISE:
But didn't you do that yesterday?

AGNES:
I missed a spot.

LOUISE:
Oh. You okay?

AGNES:
Wonderful. Are you going somewhere?

LOUISE:
Yeah I'm going to—

AGNES:
'Kay. Bye.

LOUISE:
Bye.

> *LOUISE exits. She meets THERESA in the doorway as THERESA enters. LOUISE gestures to THERESA that AGNES is in a foul mood.*

THERESA:
I'm back.

AGNES:
That's nice.

AGNES continues to scrub as THERESA stands watching her.

THERESA:

What are you trying to do, get far enough into the grain so you can count the rings?

AGNES:

It's therapeutic.

THERESA:

You should try getting out of the house. It's a lovely day.

AGNES:

Thanks for the advice and the weather report.

THERESA:

It's such a beautiful island. We so take it for granted living here, we don't really see it.

AGNES:

Tell it to the Tourist Bureau.

THERESA:

Neil's Harbour. Ingonish. And poor old Meat Cove—very misunderstood, quite wonderful really. And Cape North.

AGNES:

What are you talking about?

THERESA:

Took a little drive around this morning.

AGNES:

To Cape North?

THERESA:

I heard they had a nice craft shop there.

AGNES:
Theresa ...

THERESA:
Not a very pleasant lady running it though.

AGNES:
Theresa ...

THERESA:
I saw her. Joanie.

AGNES:
What?

THERESA:
Didn't take too long to find her. It's a small enough place. I recognized her right off by your description. She seems nice.

AGNES:
What? You talked to her?

THERESA:
Oh yes. A very outgoing girl.

AGNES:
Who ... What ... Who did you say you were?

THERESA:
I introduced myself as the sister of her friend Agnes. She mentioned that she'd missed you not being around lately.

AGNES:
You're the limit you really are.

THERESA:
Well I thought I should meet her if I'm going to be spending so much time with her.

AGNES:
What?

THERESA:
I think she should be here.

AGNES:
Oh so what, you're stepping in to save the day?

THERESA:
Agnes—

AGNES:
I suggest it and it's a no, and then you decide you're going to be the good Christian—the selfless Samaritan.

THERESA:
Let's not fight.

AGNES:
Are you just trying to torture me? To drive me crazy?

THERESA:
I prayed on it.

AGNES:
Oh, and what did the Boss have to say about it?

THERESA:
Nothing. Which I took as a good sign. When God starts talking you know you're in for trouble.

AGNES:
I see.

THERESA:
But one thing I did think was, when you get to the end of the road you can either turn around and go back the way you came—or you can make a new path.

AGNES:

A new path?

THERESA:

A new path.

AGNES:

A path straight to Cape North.

THERESA:

I just thought alright I'll go up and have a look
around and see what the situation is. And you're
right. It's not good.

AGNES:

Three days ago I wasn't capable and now all of a
sudden—

THERESA:

I'm not saying that you are capable, but surely
between the three of us we can manage.

AGNES:

Yeah well I'm not so sure anymore.

THERESA:

Louise and I are her aunts after all.

AGNES:

I have to think about it.

THERESA:

Well you've got till Saturday to think about it
because that's when I said we were coming up to get
her.

AGNES:

What? Without asking me?

THERESA:

It was your idea.

AGNES:

But you said ... Oh, honest to God I could just ...
No. No. You can't do this. You can't just turn
around like that and ... No. Anyway I'm thinking
about going back to Toronto soon. This was all
just ... stupid. I was stupid to think that things could
work out. The damage is done and that's that.
Stupid as ever.

THERESA:

Agnes?

AGNES:

New path my eye.

THERESA:

Agnes? You're going to need a machete for this one.

AGNES:

What?

THERESA:

The path gets a bit thick here.

AGNES:

What are you talking about?

THERESA:

She's pregnant.

AGNES:

What?

THERESA:

She just found out. She thought she might be but
she just found out for sure.

AGNES:

Oh my God.

THERESA:

Two months along. And she wants the baby but she's not taking care of herself. She needs some help. We have no choice but to do it. And that that ... arse of a boyfriend he's just left her high and dry.

AGNES:

A machete? Try a chainsaw.

THERESA:

She'll be fine. We'll take care of her.

AGNES:

Forget the chainsaw. Bring on the bulldozers.

THERESA:

And anyway, if there's anything that'll settle you down it's being a grandmother.

AGNES:

Dynamite! We're going to need dynamite! Good Lord! I'm too young to be a grandmother.

THERESA:

That's what happens when you start dealing with unconventional girls. Grandma.

AGNES:

Stop that. Oh my God, a grandmother. I'm not even used to being a mother yet. Oh my Lord ... Is this going to work? Is this ... Can we do this Theresa?

THERESA:

Well I was thinking about it on the way home and I figured the best thing to do is just pretend it's a movie and hope for a happy ending.

AGNES:

No this is real. This is really real.

THERESA:
Yes I guess it is, Grandma.

AGNES:
Stop it!

THERESA:
(*runs out laughing*) Grandma!

AGNES:
(*running out after her*) You're evil!

THERESA:
(*off*) Grandma!

AGNES:
(*off*) Stop it!

Scene Six

> *AGNES stands looking out. THERESA crosses the stage carrying sandwiches.*

THERESA:
Any sign?

AGNES:
Not yet.

What have you got there?

THERESA:
Sandwiches for the drive.

> *THERESA exits.*

AGNES:
(*sarcastically*) Sure we'll make a picnic of it.

THERESA re-enters.

AGNES:
> I'm scared out of my wits.

THERESA:
> That's only human.

AGNES:
> I've got to tell her. Who I am.

THERESA:
> There's no rush. You'll know when the time is right.

AGNES:
> I told Sandy she's coming.

THERESA:
> And what did Sandy say?

AGNES:
> Oh he started blubbering.

THERESA:
> That's sweet.

AGNES:
> More like pathetic I'd say. What's going to happen to poor Sandy?

THERESA:
> He'll be alright, he's got Charlie.

THERESA:
> Yes I guess.

AGNES:
> There's someone coming.

THERESA:
> That's not Louise.

AGNES:
Yes it is.

THERESA:
Well what's she doing driving that big thing?

AGNES:
It sure is red.

THERESA:
It's huge.

LOUISE enters.

LOUISE:
Isn't she beautiful!

THERESA:
What is it?

LOUISE:
Isn't she beautiful!

THERESA:
Where's our car?

LOUISE:
That's our new car.

THERESA:
That's not a car.

LOUISE:
It's our new truck.

THERESA:
Where'd it come from?

LOUISE:
I bought it off Dory.

THERESA:
What?

LOUISE:
Agnes said I should.

THERESA:
She did?

AGNES:
I did?

LOUISE:
Yeah we had a talk and she said if there was something I wanted then it was right and that I'd know inside what I needed to do.

THERESA:
(*to AGNES*) You did?

AGNES:
Well … yes … I guess I did.

LOUISE:
And you said I should get us a new car.

THERESA:
That's not a car.

LOUISE:
I know! Isn't she beautiful!

THERESA:
I'm not going to be able to drive that rig it's as big as a house.

LOUISE:
It's easy, she handles like nothing.

THERESA:
I'll feel like a farmer.

AGNES:
You are a farmer.

THERESA:

Oh, yes, well I suppose I am.

LOUISE:

You're going to love her.

THERESA:

Well come on then, truck, car, whatever we should go if we're going.

AGNES:

Oh Lord … What time did you say we'd be there?

THERESA:

About four.

AGNES:

Four? That's half a day away!

THERESA:

Yes I know, we're going to take a little detour on the way.

AGNES:

I don't know if I can handle another detour.

The women start out. They continue to talk as they exit.

LOUISE:

As long as we're back in time for Theresa's show.

THERESA:

It's not my show. I haven't even looked at it in days.

LOUISE:

Oh it's getting really good again.

THERESA:

I don't even want to know.

AGNES:

Yesterday was excellent.

LOUISE:
Oh yeah I love seeing Kara get hers.

THERESA:
She did?

LOUISE:
Yeah and good.

THERESA:
Are the aliens gone?

LOUISE:
Yeah they're back to real stuff now.

Scene Seven

The three women stand on a beach in Marion Bridge.

AGNES:
Oh this isn't how I remember it at all.

THERESA:
It's built up quite a bit.

AGNES:
They paved the road at least.

THERESA:
Look at that big place.

AGNES:
Americans probably.

LOUISE:
Not much of a bridge.

THERESA:

No indeed—you think if they named it after a bridge it'd be a bit nicer bridge.

AGNES:

I'm sure it was a beautiful bridge before Progress got his hands on it.

THERESA:

Indeed.

LOUISE:

I wonder what Mother loved so much about it here?

AGNES:

Not the rocky old beach that's for sure.

THERESA:

No it was that.

AGNES:

What?

THERESA:

The sky. That day we came out and it was so beautiful at first.

LOUISE:

I never came.

THERESA:

No but you could've.

LOUISE:

I had the chicken pox!

THERESA:

Two weeks before. You were fine. You just wanted to stay home because Deena Jessome was coming over to babysit you.

LOUISE:
Get outa here. I never even liked her.

THERESA:
You were always following her around. What you didn't like was her boyfriends.

LOUISE:
Yeah? Maybe ...

THERESA:
It was a lovely day.

AGNES:
That's not how I remember it.

THERESA:
No you were too busy chasing that poor little dog down the beach and tormenting him. It's a wonder he didn't bite you.

AGNES:
He did!

THERESA:
Yes I know that's your story but what happened was you stepped on a nail chasing the poor little thing.

AGNES:
Oh yeah.

THERESA:
It was lovely. Mother was so happy. Just staring out at the sky, lost in her dreams. But Dad didn't like that, no, he never liked seeing Mother content, and he started in on her. Just after that it started to rain. The rain followed us all the way home. And then it stopped. And then the four of us, us and Mother, we stood out in the backyard and saw the rainbow.

AGNES:
  The rainbow.

LOUISE:
  Oh yeah.

THERESA:
  Filled the whole sky. My goodness look at it ... So
  big out here. Like you could just touch it.

LOUISE:
  Yeah.

THERESA:
  Just touch it like that.

LOUISE:
  Look at the clouds.

THERESA:
  Mmmm.

LOUISE:
  Oh look at that one!

AGNES:
  Which one?

LOUISE:
  That one there. It's a girl. See her? With her arm
  up?

AGNES:
  Oh yeah.

THERESA:
  Where?

AGNES:
  She's swimming.

THERESA:
  Where?

LOUISE:
No she's riding a horse.

AGNES:
I don't see the horse.

THERESA:
I don't see the girl.

LOUISE:
There. With the long hair and her arm up—and
look a little smile.

THERESA:
Oh yes.

AGNES:
Where's the horse?

THERESA:
Right under her—see that big piece is the head
and—

AGNES:
Oh yes I see it.

THERESA:
Look at that.

LOUISE:
She's happy.

AGNES:
Riding away riding away riding away.

LOUISE:
Riding away.

THERESA:
She's flying.

LOUISE:
She is.

AGNES:
  She's flying.

> *THERESA takes a huge pile of yellow post-it notes from
> her pocket. She hands a bunch to LOUISE.*

THERESA:
  Here.

LOUISE:
  You saved them.

> *THERESA hands a bunch to AGNES and keeps a
> bunch for herself.*

THERESA:
  To the sky. For mother.

> *The three women throw the notes high into the air.
> They stand each with an arm above their head as the
> notes fall around them and the lights fade.*

End